Evy Sackrider (née Grace) was born and raised in Kirkland Lake, Ontario. She has lived in Kearns, Virginiatown, Armistice, Orillia, and Simcoe, Ontario in Canada. She is 80 years young on Boxing Day, December 26th, 2023. Evy was married for 57 years to Henry, and they had three children – Lisa, Allan, and Charles. She has had a wonderful life believing in God, where everything is possible. She loved her parents, loves her children and nature, walking her dog, writing, music, sports, and being kind to others and having a sense of humor. She owned SAX VIDEO & VARIETY in Kirkland Lake, Ontario. She was a registered Realtor and also a Broker of Record of SAX Real Estate Brokerage in Norfolk County for a total of 25 years, before retiring in her 79th year.

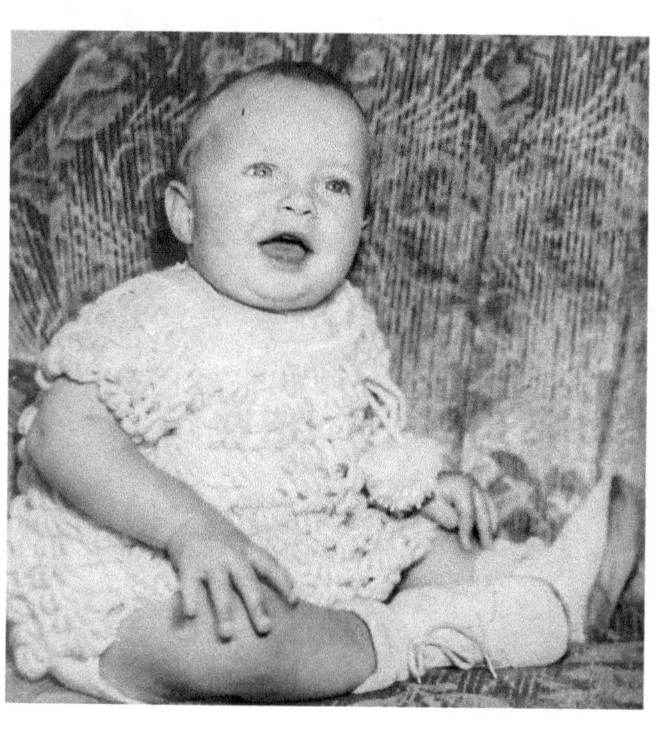

I wish to dedicate *To Touch a Heart* to my wonderful parents,
Al and Edith Grace.

Evy Sackrider

To Touch a Heart

AUSTIN MACAULEY PUBLISHERS™

LONDON • CAMBRIDGE • NEW YORK • SHARJAH

Ordering Information
Quantity sales: Special discounts are available on quantity purchases by corporations, associations, and others. For details, contact the publisher at the address below.

Publisher's Cataloging-in-Publication data
Sackrider, Evy
To Touch a Heart

ISBN 9798891554023 (Paperback)
ISBN 9798891554030 (ePub e-book)

Library of Congress Control Number: 2023924424

www.austinmacauley.com/us

First Published 2024
Austin Macauley Publishers LLC
40 Wall Street, 33rd Floor, Suite 3302
New York, NY 10005
USA

mail-usa@austinmacauley.com
+1 (646) 5125767

Table of Contents

To Touch a Heart

To touch a heart
and then part
From this life
Is like a knife
Piercing a point
To anoint
My soul
With a whole
Lot of love
Sent from above
To remember and cherish
Time with your loved one and wish
You happiness when you're apart
And pride that she knew how to touch a heart.

A Bee in My Bonnet

There was something
About the bumble bee
That gave me a zing
to see
Just how many I could capture.

The rapture
of their color
Bold shades of orange and yellow
powder
Banded with black.

I eavesdropped through the nail hole
And the buzz word was attack
So being a kind soul
I set them free
Preventing a bee in my bonnet.

Cheminis Hill

It was a long way to the top.
I was okay
as I was with Pop.
You hung onto the side
Or you'd tilt way back.
From the top the ride
Went the length of a mini-track.
I was secured by his hand
At the end of the rein
My daddy manned
If momentum would gain.
The thrill of it all
Passed many a winter night.
Daddy made me feel tall
And high as a kite.
It was such a simple thing to do
And fresh air
To banish a winter blue.
The zip of Cheminis Hill, a dare.

Daddy's Girl

I loved to sit with Daddy
While he puffed his White Owl
I, a wee lassie
He with a thirtyish scowl
Silence was broken
By a plane roaring above
My inquisitive token
To enquire about Auntie
being a Wren
To the war just past
Then there was a firecracker blast
To mark the celebration
of Dominion Day fun.

Fun in the Dark

We turned out the light.
All systems go.
There wasn't even a fight
As we lay low.
Turned on the switch
and it started its cycle.
At a crossing we'd hitch
Another car on to tickle our fancy.
The light of the engine
Headed the wee train
which chugged to the coal bin.
A whistle would sound
To warn of the oncoming train.
A white lantern glowed round
The corner as we gain
Speed and then cruise
The rest of the way
and lose momentum to stay
at the station for the night.
We had fun
on our fantasy flight.

Larder Lake

The sky was gray
and we were past the bay
In this big canoe
Which could tip on cue
The swells were deep
To make my heart leap.
Does this ever end?
Shore's around the next bend.
The picnic was fun
but now that it's done
I want to get safely home
and out of this foam.
You feel like a swirl
down a drain, girl
and then a bobber
rising up to clobber.
The grasp of this lake
which has given many a wake.

Armistice

I love to be close to nature
So I was sure happy to move to
the site of Armistice,
in a new home by the lake
where blood suckers make you leery to swim there.
I found another dare
to keep me busy.
I'd step off the cement pillar and grasp
and sliding right, then left, I'd clasp
the iron bar which seemed far
to the next resting place
to slow down my pace.
I found baby frogs by the ton
Placed them in my Mother's sink, no pun.
I learned balance walking a slippery pipe
and jumping off into berries ripe.
We gathered smooth slippery sticks
and peer down a dark hole for kicks.
We'd run all around this deserted mine
Set in the midst of forest pine.
Many days I walked the twisted road, bold
Observing the seasons unfold.
Years later this same mine is doing just fine.
My vision of piles of gold
was called Armistice, my stronghold.

Living in a Fishbowl

I was only nine when we moved
to the city of gold talking swine.
My parents borrowed from their kitty
to purchase their dream
A confectionery store…
Life wasn't always all cream but it wasn't a bore.
Momma was always there
when I crossed the street
to share my day and I'd greet her customers too.
Some regulars, others by chance.
The regulars knew our daily life
and enhance our spirits to grow
during times of strife or joy.
There was always a steady flow
of opinions to employ.
The buyer shared my first two-wheeler,
my public speaking honor, my first date.
Cupid the dealer dealt me my present mate.
They all noticed a new pimple
and watched me turn into bait.
Life wasn't simple.
When I graduated our Store was sold.
I shared a bed with a husband to hold.
Life goes on, a bigger care…
A motel, a new goal for my parents to share,
who loved living in a fishbowl.

Wee Willy

His nickname, wee Willy
stood for Billy
This little boy
with a ship for a toy
headed for the creek
with high rubber boots, to seek
so much pleasure, from water,
the lure…
He'd sail the ship
'til he took a slip
Then home he'd go
to change clothes so
He and his ship, a team
Could dream downstream.

A Garden of Love

Ladders of string made a lattice
for green stems to grow tall.
Different shades threw a springtime kiss
as the flowers crawled the wall.
A bare space filled with beauty
met the wandering eye
that wished to see
those sweet peas as they passed by.

Vulgar Words

Vulgar words are not new.
They've been around for ages.
They evolve at certain stages
by a chosen few
especially a young fellow
I thought was a fool
on the school rooftop, he'd pool
these words and bellow
Father, Uncle, Cousin, King.
I didn't have a clue
Why those words stuck like glue
and had an unusual ring.

Crystal Beach

Our wakeup call was after the rising sun.
I sauntered down the hall.
Today was to be fun!

We only met the odd car on the route there
which was par for the hour fair.

To share a family swim when everyone could go.
We had to quash a whim of sunbathing full quo.

We parked the car.
We had a private spot.
The mud wouldn't jar as it wasn't hot.

Over the track and down the path
The beach had a lack of people to sunbathe.

It's not the same on an empty beach
No one came if you got a leech.

The air had a nip. The water was cool.
No one taking a dip in this beautiful pool.

It's more fun with a mass
but quality time of one family, left a memory with class.

Tomstown

We stayed at Tomstown
for many a day.
My brother and I would clown
around in the stack of hay,
rather picky to say the least.
Then we'd head to the river
to drop a line and dream of a fish feast.
The noon day sun made us quiver.
Time to head home to eat.
The race back was spent
ducking a cow paddie, quite a feat!
After eating, we both went
to pile wood by the cord.
I could vision the snakes in the grass.
Heads up high and bored,
waiting to move in by the mass
in our neat woodpile.
Oh how I loved piling that wood!
It was time to rest awhile.
I was always good
but I loved to read
to the end of the book.
Good advice I didn't heed…
Putting a cover over the lamp took
only a few minutes to burst into flame.
Then the whole house was awake
and everyone came before we'd all bake.
Got that flame out.
Enough excitement for one day!
I'll dream of another trick, no doubt,
like shaving cream for mayonnaise, not okay…
Being a Farm Girl for awhile
was a breath of fresh air,
excitement by the mile
and life without a care!

Ted

Ted, to many folk
Was the whistling mailman.
To me, he would evoke
A love of nature, Canadian.
After Sunday School
I'd run home to ask
and get store cookies to pool
with homemade ones as we'd bask
in the sunshine
in the forest.
After we'd walk the line
with Ted's imagination, the best,
till we found our secret patch
of the biggest berries, blue
and when our baskets would match,
we'd eat and feel anew
for the march home
with our berries to the rim
we'd roam,
full of vigor and vim.

Federal Rink

I'd toe pick
so no nick
would warp my blade
as I made
my way across the street
where I would meet
The Plager boys
who used pucks for toys.
Me, in my fancy dress
would the ice caress
amidst hard slaps on the board
and an echo that roared.
When toes would tingle,
into the Rink Shack I'd mingle.
By the warmth of the hot metal
which could drop any petal.
You'd see the odd steaming sock
from one of the flock
and a written love connection
burnt on the wooden wall in fun.
In my past, what a link!
That old Federal Rink.

Fish Face Grace

Was the only graffiti
Written about me
on the door
of our Corner Store
across from the School.
I didn't think it was cool…
Almost a decade
my parents made
our living to exist
and we had a list
of many a good friend
who signed a card to send
us best wishes in our farewell
and gave us a clock to tell
the world their pride
of being side by side.

Sounds of Yesteryear

One long, two short
Two short, one long
Not our ring, so you abort
your listening ear to the song
on the upright radio.
After, I found the key
to play do, re, me, do
on the piano before me.
Then the sound of hooves
distracted me to go watch
the horses clip clop moves
and swishing tails botch
the flight of the horsefly.
There's the squeaking of the pump,
the well never ran dry.
I hear the tin watering cans bump
as it's time to freshen up the gardens.
As I pass the outhouse door,
someone's ripping newspaper by the tens.
Scrubbing clothes on rippled glass wore
your fingers to the bone.
Sounds of yesteryear I'd loan.

A Buck in the System

I was a tender age
when I learned a page
may contain a word which is sour as curd.
Like my friendly wave I gave the stranger.
Gramma said, "no."
A shopping trip made my Gramma flip.
I wanted the colored doll in the 5 & 10 stall.
Rest time after noon meal
meant the trunk held appeal.
To cast off stockings, long and white
for anklets was a fight.
The piano was locked.
I found the key and rocked.
I was fascinated by the girl on rubble for her bed,
my imagination it fed.
Grampa took the book of war away
before I wanted more.
Let's go for the mail
and even after the tale
of the train hitting the lady smack,
I'd still walk on the track.
Life was an adventure which was hard to cure.

By the Grace of a Swede

I'm the little girl
who let the bubbles swirl
through the plastic wand.
The bond
I had was through my dad
and I'm so glad
they called it Swede town then
but I was only ten.

I'm the little girl
in this rural area
who tore around the house for
the approaching train,
sunshine or rain.
To the conductor I'd wave
and he gave me a wave back.
I wondered what was down the track.

By the Grace of a Swede
(continued)

I'm the little girl
who gave gardening a whirl.
I'd help Grampaw
with tending vegetables raw
or pick the potato bug
or odd slug.
We'd check each row
for anything which shouldn't grow.
Then we'd rest under the tree
As happy as can be.

I'm the little girl
with the wet curl
from splashing in the square tub
where Gramma gave the washing a scrub.
On the days you bake
I'd glance across at the lake.
I'd pump and pump
to see well water dump
into my pail.
My method would never fail.
I'd wave to a gentleman
who stooped low with a pan
And knew a good spring to go to.

Gramma Grace

She wore her long hair
braided in a bun style.
Long, it rippled with flair
as she preened for awhile.

She always wore a flowery frock
and modesty prevailed.
A bodice brooch would mock,
a bosom jailed.

She loved her role in life
of Mother and devoted wife.
Busy fingers toiled all day,
never thinking "Where's my pay?"

Even the smallest task
was of monumental importance.
Whether scrubbing clothes
in the sun's bask
or airing pillows,
to odor lance.

A curtain was the pantry's entry.
A special place to go.
An array of sweets to free
the adrenalin to flow.

Gramma Grace (continued)

She'd whet the lead
and write up her grocery list.
Then give instructions to Ed
who'd get the gist.

Moments of relaxation
were spent together
Under the oak which visored the sun
for our family encounter.

Rest time after the noon meal
"was for my own good," she said.
That was when I'd steal
memories from the trunk by my bed.

As dusk blotted day,
steam seeping from the reservoir seam
signaled a bath and a pleasant dream.

Grampa Grace

When I became thirteen,
A new phase of life began.
After two seasons had been,
into my life came a man.
He was old and wise
and had just buried his wife.
It was a nice surprise!
He was coming to spend the rest of his life
with our family of four,
a dog named Penny,
a bird and a Store,
all for him to oversee.
He had many a tale to tell
and I was his audience.
Down a mineshaft 70 feet he fell
onto rock, a limp hence.
He survived the fire of Haileybury,
ashes were all that remained of his home.
He weathered another fury,
the Porcupine fire where he'd roam
into water up to his neck
to save his soul.

Grampa Grace (continued)

The match factory did deck
his hearing which took a toll.
He taught me tricks
and turned his hearing aid off
to sing me his favorite picks
off key and I'd never scoff.
He had walked a tightrope.
He taught me the Swedish language.
He touched my head and gave me hope.
He walked when on his rampage.
His passion was Mom's meal.
Sometimes life held a heartsick gauge…
I'm glad I got to feel
Blessed in the human race
to have shared life with Grampa Grace.

October 4, 1922

It was a normal day
after a Summer, hot and dry.
The sky grew dark west way,
thought it was a rainstorm coming by.

Off two years from a shaft fall,
Dad was back at the mine.
Mother and Esther papered the wall
while supper simmered fine.

At 4:30, Dad rushed home,
said Haileybury was burning,
tied the cows so they wouldn't roam,
flagged a coal truck turning.

The wind would zig zag
igniting things in its path.
A flaming haystack played tag
as the fire dealt its wrath.

We spent the night in Cobalt Station.
A wind shift spared Cobalt.
Some people went the Toronto run
as the railway ties burnt to a halt.

October 4, 1922 (continued)

Lucky my sister got the mail.
North Cobalt Post Office burnt to the ground.
The Workmen's Compensation cheque would bail
us out from being poverty bound.

The next day there was snow!
I walked down Lang Street
to have breakfast with people I didn't know
and survey the damage from the heat.

Steel girders looked like a U Turn.
Our home was a pile of ash.
Our family plus orphaned children were our concern.
Stayed at Petersen's,
then a shack for a little cash.

At bedtime, we dressed warmer.
All nails had frost on their head.
Frost on the blanket we'd endure
'til the fire was lit by Ed.

For Eaton's and Simpson's we're grateful
as we only had the clothes on our back.
Neighbors helped neighbors pull
through the turmoil with knack.

10,000 homeless and forty-four dead.
$8,000,000 loss in property.
The government and Red Cross fed
relief to burning bush victims like me.

A Green Thumb

I couldn't imagine
a green thumb
but one of my kin
could succumb.
Dear Gramma
Worked her barren soil.
It's nature's law if you toil,
you reap what you sow.
I was amazed
at the vegetables she grew
from stooping low
just after the dew.
I watched her pat
and weed a flower
and when Grampa and I sat
we saw her spring dower.
I can remember the porch facing east
full of geraniums pure,
a savory feast.
She wasn't dumb.
She had a green thumb.

Effie

He called me Effie.
A Shawville name I guess,
close enough to suit me
I must confess.
He loved to be a Joker
and played his cards well.
Many a kitten did purr
from his influential spell.

When his mining days were done,
he scraped snow at the rink.
To be involved with kids was fun
and kept him in the pink.
We'd sit side by side
on a Summer's eve,
filled with pride
and our hearts on our sleeve.

Always

I'll be yours forever
until our ties sever.
In the good times
or if sorrow chimes,
cause that's what it's all about.
Never doubt
all your days
My friendship, always.

True Love

True love stems from the womb.
Conceived by va, va, voom.
An entrance.
A loving glance.
A tender touch
means much.
In the beginning of life
less strife
to become a living label
and fable.
To be strong and survive
and derive
the most pleasure
to measure
our life spent on Earth
and our human worth

The Imprint on the Door

As I go forth
in the direction North
My eyes scan
for the man
sitting in front of his door
on the ground floor.
Eyes off in space,
A cigarette in his face,
always huddled on all four,
his ship always at shore.
Some people have an effect
when they defect.
He's missing in action
but only a fraction.
This landmark left the scene
not clean
As the oil from his body pore
left the imprint on the door.

Birds of a Feather

A couple from the human race
who've never seen each other's face,
their ages separated by a gap
and homes nearby on a map
are similar in many ways
as they've spent many days
writing to their heart's desire,
fueled by a non-fiction fire
of an energetic life
conquering strife
and adjusted with age
to plume another page
before life slips away
as their words won't decay.

A Write-Off

Thinking about it,
I'm glad I never quit.
This guy owed me a fee
which he didn't wish to pay.
On contact, he'd say,
I'll be in on such and such a date.
I knew it was a line to wait
and delay
but I was sick of this replay.
I had resources that were accurate
and used a little wit.
If I'd sent a letter,
he'd say he didn't get it.
If I'd phone,
he'd pick a bone
and slam the blower down.
Decided to march across town
to visit the jerk
who raised my perk.
I found the even number
and looked for his name
on the box,
the newspaper drapery
advertised for free.

A Write-Off (continued)

I searched for a light
to aid my plight.
I stood my ground
as he answered my dainty pound.
The sweet smell of his success
and polluted air would mess
his success.
As I thought no more, but less
of this foolish soul
Whose lifestyle would take its toll
so I decided to abort
as the wheel of life
would deal
with this write-off.

Out of Control

It's sad
and makes me mad
when someone has a bout
of booze in and brains out.
One moment
spent
out of control
would make me set a goal
to want to change
the range
of emotions
or potions
that made me go
so
out of control.

From Vein to Vein

The registry line was long.
Every person penned a form.
Excited maybe I don't belong
as they shuttled me to the dorm.
The fast screening meant no wrong.
A sample was given, result norm.
I sat filled with song.
Next meant me in perfect form.
My heart pumping until a gong
struck to storm
me over for a rest, not long,
then sip a tea and conform
that giving blood made me strong.

A Dark Eyed Stranger

It was dark as I passed
them in the distance.
The evening sky was complete
as this stranger and I meet.
He was having an amicable chat.
I saw the slight turn of his hat.
He was dark eyed
but spied
as I passed by.
This guy had an effect
if I wished to defect.
I felt no danger
with this dark eyed stranger.

Unconditional Love

Her heart set the pace
for the smile on her face
for a job well done
and a whole lot of fun
to all who attended
who were well fed
by busy hands which made
delicacies laid
on the table.
Her label
is Speedy Edie
who prepared the Birthday Bash
with a whole lot of dash
for the Birthday Boy
who shone with joy
because in his heart
the most luscious tart
was the one sent from above
to contract with unconditional love.

Too Pooped to Pop

We all know that saying
Too pooped to pop
after a night of partying,
we feel like a flop.
I had to drive home afar.
The sun told me it was day.
I reached for my shades in the car.
With shades over my eyes, day
turned to night
which gave me such a fright
and made my nerves fray.

Every hour on the hour
I'd get a whiff of fresh air
to tap my tower
of strength in this rare
form I was in
and give me power.
A wasted day lay before me
for soon I'd stop
and be
Too pooped to pop.

Her First Bikini

She wasn't even a year
and had no fear
of wearing her bikini
for the whole world to see.
It was a hot summer day.
Workmen whistled at this little ray
of sunshine, who looked just fine.
This platinum blonde
who was so fond
of putting on the ritz
and painting the town by blitz.

He Left His Mark

The scratch marks are explosive.
Some like tic, tac, toe.
Clumps of them give
way to the odd side one, low
and then they reach above the knob
or curve for the artistic touch.
He did a good job,
to show how much
he wanted to be with me
but I was busy as a bee.
So I closed the door
which soon would bore
him to create a masterpiece
to match the one at home.
It puts a new lease
on the old door, like a dome
which caps the dullness
of boring brown.
I must confess,
it makes you smile, not frown.

Kirkland Lake

I'm from Kirkland Lake
The town that had a lake
I may be getting old
but my heart is full of gold.
I am rough on the edge
but I don't sit on the hedge.
My Northern heritage
Lived in a gilded cage
Made other folks quiz
to see what made me fizz.
I've become a carbon copy
of my poppy
due to fresh air
not a care
Family fare
and the luck of a hare
And wherever I may roam
Kirkland Lake is my home.